Superfood Cookbook: Fa
QUINOA REC
for Easy Weight Los

by Alissa Noel Grey

Table Of Contents

Amazing Quinoa Recipes the Whole Family Will Love!

Eating healthy food doesn't have to be unpleasant or time consuming. Sometimes we are a little suspicious of anything that gets touted as a 'superfood' and we often stay away from foreign foods that have been getting all the hype. That is why it took me a while to get around to trying out quinoa. Well, I now know what I've been missing!

My family and I have fallen in love with quinoa and I can simply say that it is really one of the most delicious healthy foods on the planet. In addition, quinoa is one of the of easiest ingredients to prepare. It is an important superfood you can add to your everyday menu without any effort or doubt.

What makes quinoa one of my family's favorite foods is not the fact that, according to numerous scientific research articles, it has magical superfood healing and rejuvenating qualities. If I have to be honest, what makes it top of the list for me, is the fact that it can be easily incorporated in all our old favorite dishes. Quinoa is really simple to cook even for inexperienced cooks.

What is even more amazing about this tiny grain is that the processes of boiling, simmering, or steaming do not appear to significantly compromise the quality of its fatty acids and all its other superfood qualities!

What Exactly is Quinoa?

Quinoa is the tiny grain of a staple crop in South America, primarily grown in the Andes, and has been famed since ancient Inca times. It has a mild, nutty flavor and a light, fluffy texture, and is the only plant food that is at the same time gluten-free, has a very high protein content, and contains all nine essential amino acids.

Quinoa is not only high in protein, but also rich in vitamins such as riboflavin, calcium, vitamin E, iron, potassium, phosphorus, magnesium, folic acid and beta carotene. Quinoa is great for detoxification as it has prebiotic nutrients that help feed the good bacteria in our intestine and thus prevent infections and fight back disease-causing bacteria. Recent studies have confirmed that quinoa is a natural source of lots of anti-inflammatory phytonutrients so, if you suffer from inflammation-related problems, including obesity, then quinoa is the right food for you.

And last but not least, we should remember that quinoa is gluten-free so it can be used by people trying to follow a gluten-free diet either for medical reasons or simply because they feel they don't need or like wheat products.

The recipes in my book are strictly gluten-free: I have carefully checked for gluten containing ingredients as I am also following a gluten-free diet to combat some minor health problems

Why is Quinoa So Easy To Cook?

If you've got 15 minutes, you have time to cook quinoa. It cooks up like rice only faster – wash it well, boil it and voila - you can prepare an amazing healthy salad, soup, stew, casserole, chili or curry for dinner in no time at all. Or you can toss some nuts and fruits into boiled quinoa and serve as breakfast porridge. You can include quinoa in smoothies, pancakes, cookies, puddings or muffins and then you will have not only tasty but fantastically healthy meals in your everyday menu.

To cook quinoa, all one has to do is add one part of the grain to two parts liquid in a saucepan. Bring to the boil, reduce the heat to a simmer and cover. In 15 minutes your perfect quinoa is done. Fluff with a fork and enjoy!

Quinoa Salads and Sides

Quinoa Green Salad

Serves: 4

Prep time: 5 min

Ingredients:

5-6 green lettuce leaves, washed and drained

1 cucumber, peeled and diced

1 carrot, grated

1-2 spring onions, finely cut

1 cup cooked quinoa

3 tbsp lemon juice

3 tbsp extra virgin olive oil

salt, to taste

Directions:

Cut the lettuce into thin strips. Combine it with the cucumber, carrot, spring onions and quinoa.

Combine all ingredients well and drizzle with lemon juice and olive oil. Season with salt to taste and serve.

Warm Beet and Quinoa Salad

Serves: 4

Prep time: 10 min

Ingredients:

1/2 cup cooked quinoa

1 14 oz can sliced pickled beets, drained

1/2 red onion, chopped

2 garlic cloves, crushed

6 oz feta cheese, crumbled

1 tbsp extra virgin olive oil

for the dressing

2 tbsp extra virgin olive oil

2 tbsp lemon juice

salt and black pepper, to taste

Directions:

Heat one tablespoon of olive oil in a frying pan and gently sauté onion for 2-3 minutes or until softened.

Add in garlic and beets and cook, stirring, for 2 minutes. Add half a cup of cooked quinoa.

Whisk together remaining olive oil, lemon juice, salt and pepper. Add to the quinoa mixture and toss to coat. Top with feta cheese, toss gently to combine, and serve.

Avocado, Quinoa and Red Pepper Salad

Serves: 4-5

Prep time: 6-7 min

Ingredients:

2 avocados, peeled and diced

1 cup cooked quinoa

2 red bell peppers, diced

1-2 spring onions, finely chopped

1 garlic clove, minced

3 tbsp chopped fresh coriander

3 tbsp lemon juice

2 tbsp extra virgin olive oil

½ tsp cumin

Directions:

Place avocados, quinoa, bell peppers, spring onions, garlic, coriander and cumin in a salad bowl.

Sprinkle with lemon juice and olive oil, toss to combine and serve.

Quinoa Tabbouleh

Serves 6

Prep time: 15 min

Ingredients:

1 cup cooked quinoa

2 cups fresh parsley, finely cut

1/2 cup fresh mint leaves, finely cut

2 tomatoes, chopped

7-8 spring onions, chopped

3 tbsp extra virgin olive oil

2 garlic cloves, crushed

juice of one lemon

salt and black pepper, to taste

Directions:

In a large bowl, mix together the parsley, mint, tomatoes, garlic, spring onions, lemon juice, and olive oil.

Stir well and add in quinoa.

Season to taste with salt and black pepper and toss to combine. Serve chilled.

Easy Artichoke and Quinoa Salad

Serves: 5-6

Prep time: 15 min

Ingredients:

1/2 cup cooked quinoa

1 large handful podded broad beans

3 marinated artichoke hearts, quartered

for the dressing:

2 tbsp extra virgin olive oil

2 tbsp lemon juice

1 tbsp fresh mint, chopped

salt and pepper, to taste

Directions:

Cook the broad beans in boiling, unsalted water for 2-3 minutes or until tender. Drain and refresh under running cold water.

Combine with quinoa and quartered marinated artichoke hearts in a large salad bowl.

In a smaller bowl, whisk olive oil, lemon juice, vinegar and mint. Pour over the bean mixture. Season with salt and pepper and toss gently to combine.

Quinoa and Avocado Salad

Serves: 4

Prep time: 15 min

Ingredients:

1 cup cooked quinoa

2 cups water

1 large avocado, pitted and sliced

¼ radicchio, finely sliced

1 small pink grapefruit, peeled and finely cut

a handful of arugula

1 cup baby spinach leaves

2 tbsp extra virgin olive oil

2 tbsp lemon juice

salt and black pepper, to taste

Directions:

In a salad bowl, combine avocado, radicchio, arugula, baby spinach and cooked quinoa.

Add in grapefruit, lemon juice, and olive oil; season with salt and black pepper and stir to combine well.

Quinoa and Carrot Salad

Serves: 4

Prep time: 15 min

Ingredients:

2 cups cooked quinoa

2 cups water

4 carrots, shredded

1 apple, peeled and shredded

1 garlic clove, chopped

3 tbsp lemon juice

2 tbsp extra virgin olive oil

salt, to taste

Directions:

In a deep salad bowl, combine the shredded carrots, apple, lemon juice, garlic, and salt.

Add in the cooked quinoa, toss to combine, and serve.

Fresh Quinoa Salad

Serves: 4-5

Prep time: 15 min

Ingredients:

2 cups cooked quinoa

2 cups water

1 large cucumber, diced

1 big tomato, diced

1 yellow pepper, chopped

10-15 arugula leaves

3 tbsp lemon juice

3 tbsp extra virgin olive oil

½ cup fresh dill, finely cut

salt and black pepper, to taste

Directions:

Combine the cooked quinoa, cucumber, tomato, yellow pepper, arugula and dill in a salad bowl.

I a smaller bowl, whisk the lemon juice, olive oil, salt and black pepper. Pour over the salad and toss to combine.

Roasted Sweet Potato and Quinoa Salad

Serves: 5-6

Prep time: 15 min

Ingredients:

1 cup cooked quinoa

2 lb sweet potatoes, peeled

1/2 cup roasted walnuts

1 cup beet, lentil or mixed sprouts

3-4 fresh basil leaves

2 tbsp extra virgin olive oil

2 tbsp balsamic vinegar

salt, to taste

Directions:

Cut the sweet potatoes into chunks and arrange on a baking sheet sprinkled with cinnamon, olive oil and a little salt and black pepper. Toss to coat well.

Bake at 350 F for 15 minutes, or until golden and crisp.

In a salad bowl, combine quinoa, sweet potatoes, sprouts and walnuts. Drizzle with balsamic vinegar and olive oil and serve.

Spring Quinoa Salad

Serves: 5-6

Prep time: 15 min

Ingredients:

1 cup cooked quinoa

5-6 green lettuce leaves, cut in thin stripes

10-15 arugula leaves

a bunch of radishes, sliced

1 cup grape or cherry tomatoes

½ cup green olives, pitted, halved

1 cup small mozzarella cheese

3-4 fresh basil leaves

2 tbsp extra virgin olive oil

2 tbsp fresh lemon juice

salt, to taste

Directions:

In a salad bowl, combine all vegetables, green olives, mozzarella and fresh basil leaves.

Add in quinoa, salt, lemon juice and olive oil, and toss to combine.

Mashed Avocado, Quinoa and Chicken Salad

Serves: 4-5

Prep time: 5 min

Ingredients:

1 cup cooked quinoa

1 cup cooked chicken breasts, diced

1 small red onion, finely chopped

2 ripe avocados, mashed with a fork

3 tbsp lemon juice

1 tbsp extra virgin olive oil

1 tbsp fresh tarragon leaves, finely cut

salt and black pepper, to taste

Directions:

Place the chicken in a medium sized salad bowl.

In a plate, mash the avocados using either a fork or a potato masher and add them to the chicken. Add in a cup of cooked quinoa, onion, tarragon, lemon juice and olive oil. Season with salt and black pepper, stir to combine, and serve.

Kid-friendly Quinoa, Chicken and Vegetable Salad

Serves: 5-6

Prep time: 5 min

Ingredients:

1 cup cooked quinoa

1 cup cooked chicken

1 carrot, boiled and diced

3 pickled gherkins, diced

1/2 cup green peas, cooked and drained

1/2 cup mayonnaise

2 tbsp Greek yogurt

salt, to taste

Directions:

Place all vegetables and chicken in a salad bowl. Add in mayonnaise and yogurt and stir until well combined.

Add a cup of cooked quinoa, toss to combine and serve.

Healthy Winter Quinoa Salad

Serves: 4

Prep time: 15 min

Ingredients:

1 cup cooked quinoa

1-2 small beets, peeled, boiled and grated

1 apple, peeled and shredded

1 small turnip, grated

3-4 spring onions, finely cut

½ bunch of fresh parsley, finely cut

2 tbsp lemon juice

1 tsp chia seeds

3 tbsp extra virgin olive oil

salt, to taste

Directions:

Steam the beets in a basket over a pot of boiling water for about 12-15 minutes, or until tender. Leave them to cool then grate and put them in a salad bowl.

Add in the finely cut spring onions, the shredded apple and turnip, and the fresh parsley. Toss to combine.

Season with salt, lemon juice and olive oil, add in quinoa and chia seeds and stir.

Quinoa, Black Bean and Egg Salad

Serves: 4-5

Prep time: 15 min

Ingredients:

2 cups cooked quinoa

1 cup canned black beans, drained

1 tomato, diced

2-3 spring onions, chopped

2 eggs, hard boiled, peeled and sliced

½ cup fresh cilantro, finely cut

1 tsp dried mint

3 tbsp lemon juice

4 tbsp extra virgin olive oil

½ tsp salt

Directions:

Put the beans, tomato, spring onions, eggs, and cilantro in a bowl and toss with lemon juice, olive oil, dried mint and salt.

Add in quinoa and toss to combine.

Baby Spinach Quinoa Salad

Serves: 4-5

Prep time: 15 min

Ingredients:

1 cup cooked quinoa

2 cups baby spinach, washed and dried

2 tomatoes, sliced

2-3 green onions, finely chopped

4 oz crumbled blue cheese

1/2 cup roasted walnuts

2 tbsp lemon juice

4 tbsp extra virgin olive oil

salt, to taste

Directions:

Place the baby spinach leaves in a large bowl and add in tomatoes, green onions and blue cheese. Stir in the quinoa and roasted walnuts.

Season to taste with salt, add the lemon juice and olive oil and stir again.

Quinoa, Kale and Roasted Pumpkin

Serves: 4-5

Prep time: 30-35 min

Ingredients:

1 cup quinoa, rinsed

1.5 lb pumpkin, peeled and seeded, cut into cubes

2 cups fresh kale, chopped

5 oz crumbled feta cheese

1 large onion, finely chopped

4-5 tbsp extra virgin olive oil

1 tsp finely grated ginger

½ tsp cumin

½ tsp salt

Directions:

Preheat the oven to 350 F. Line a baking tray and arrange the pumpkin cubes on on it. Drizzle with 2-3 tablespoons of olive oil and salt. Toss to coat, place in the oven and cook for 20-25 minutes, stirring every 10 minutes.

Heat the remaining olive oil in a large saucepan over medium-high heat. Gently sauté onion, for 2-3 minutes, or until softened. Add the spices and cook, stirring, for 1 minute more.

Wash quinoa under running water until the water runs clear. Bring two cups of water to a boil and add quinoa. Reduce heat to low, cover, and simmer for 15 minutes. Stir in kale and cook until it wilts. Gently combine quinoa and kale mixture with the roasted pumpkin and sautéed onion.

Quinoa and Brussels Sprouts Salad

Serves: 5-6

Prep time: 20-25 min

Ingredients:

2 cups cooked quinoa

4 cups Brussels sprouts, halved

2 leeks, washed, trimmed and sliced

½ cup walnuts, chopped

½ cup dried cranberries

½ cup fresh parsley, chopped

2 tbsp balsamic vinegar

3 tbsp extra virgin olive oil

Directions:

Preheat the oven to 350 F. Line a baking tray and arrange Brussels sprouts and leeks on it. Drizzle with olive oil, balsamic vinegar and salt and toss to coat. Roast about 20-25 minutes.

In a salad bowl, toss together the quinoa, roasted vegetables, walnuts and cranberries. Season with salt and pepper to taste and serve.

Warm Quinoa Salad with Broccoli and Roasted Peppers

Serves: 4

Prep time: 25 min

Ingredients:

1 cup cooked quinoa

1 small broccoli head, cut into florets

2-3 roasted bell peppers, peeled and cut in strips

1/2 red onion, finely chopped

3 garlic cloves, crushed or chopped

1 tbsp balsamic vinegar

2-3 tbsp extra virgin olive oil

½ cup fresh dill, finely cut, to serve

salt and black pepper, to taste

Directions:

Arrange broccoli on a baking sheet and drizzle with garlic, olive oil, balsamic vinegar and salt. Toss to coat. Roast in a preheated to 350 F oven for about 20 minutes, or until tender.

Transfer the broccoli in a large salad bowl along with the roasted peppers and quinoa. Stir in red onion. Sprinkle with dill, toss to combine, and serve.

Warm Mushroom and Quinoa Salad

Serves: 4

Prep time: 10 min

Ingredients:

2/3 cup cooked quinoa

5-6 spring onions, chopped

10-12 white mushrooms, sliced

1 tsp dried thyme

1 cup sun dried tomatoes, cut

¾ cup lentil sprouts (or sprouts of choice)

⅓ cup roasted almonds, chopped

2 tbsp extra virgin olive oil

salt, to taste

black pepper, optional

Directions:

Heat the olive oil in a frying pan and gently sauté the spring onions for 1-2 minutes. Stir in the mushrooms and thyme, and season with salt, to taste.

Cook, stirring, until the mushrooms soften and most of the liquid evaporates. Add in quinoa and sun dried tomatoes and stir.

Top with roasted almonds and sprouts and serve.

Quinoa and Apple Salad

Serves: 3-4

Prep time: 2-3 min

Ingredients:

1 cup cooked quinoa

1 small cucumber, peeled and diced

2 apples, cored and diced

⅓ cup dried unsweetened cherries or cranberries

¼ cup walnuts

2 tbsp extra virgin olive oil

1 tbsp balsamic vinegar

salt and pepper, to taste

Directions:

Combine all ingredients in a large salad bowl. Toss with balsamic vinegar and olive oil and season to taste with salt and pepper.

Serve chilled or at a room temperature.

Feta and Quinoa Stuffed Zucchinis

Serves 5-6

Prep time: 20 min

Ingredients:

5-6 large zucchinis, peeled

1 cup feta cheese, crumbled

1/2 cup cooked quinoa

3 eggs

1 small onion, finely chopped

1/3 cup yogurt

2 tbsp extra virgin olive oil

salt, to taste

Directions:

Halve the zucchinis lengthwise, hollow and salt them.

In a skillet, heat the olive oil and gently sauté the onion.

In a bowl, combine quinoa, feta cheese, one egg and the sautéed onion.

Stuff the zucchinis with the quinoa mixture, arrange them in a baking dish and pour over the remaining 2 eggs whisked with the yogurt.

Bake in a preheated to 350 F oven for about 20 minutes.

Quinoa Soups

Quinoa, Chicken and Bacon Soup

Serves: 6-7

Prep time: 30 min

Ingredients:

3 bacon strips, diced

2 cups chicken, cooked and shredded

1 cup quinoa, rinsed

1 onion, chopped

2 garlic cloves, crushed

5 cups water

1 cup canned tomatoes, diced, undrained

1 bay leaf

1 tsp dried thyme

½ tsp dried basil

salt and pepper, to taste

Directions:

In a deep pot, cook the onion and bacon over medium-high heat. Drain off the fat.

Add in garlic, and cook for a minute, stirring. Add in water, quinoa, tomatoes and seasonings and bring to a boil.

Cover, reduce heat, and simmer for 20 minutes. Add in the chicken, simmer for 5 minutes, and serve.

Mediterranean Chicken and Quinoa Soup

Serves: 4-5

Prep time: 30 min

Ingredients:

1.5 lb chicken breasts

2 carrots, chopped

1 celery stalk, chopped

1 red onion, chopped

1/2 cup quinoa, rinsed

5 cups water

10 black olives, pitted and halved

salt and black pepper, to taste

fresh parsley or coriander, to serve

lemon juice, to serve

Directions:

Place the chicken breasts in a deep soup pot. Add in onion, carrots, celery, salt, pepper and water. Stir well and bring to a boil.

Stir in quinoa and olives, reduce heat, and simmer for 30 minutes.

Remove chicken from the pot and let it cool slightly. Shred it and return it back to the pot.

Serve soup with lemon juice and sprinkled with fresh parsley or coriander.

Beef, Quinoa and Vegetable Minestrone

Serves: 4-5

Prep time: 30 min

Ingredients:

2 slices bacon, chopped

1 cup lean ground beef

1/2 cup quinoa, rinsed

5 cups beef broth

1 onion, chopped

1 celery stalk, chopped

1/2 cup canned chickpeas, drained

1 carrot, chopped

1 small zucchini, peeled and diced

1 garlic clove, finely chopped

1 cup canned tomatoes, chopped

1 bay leaf

1 tsp dried basil

1 tsp dried rosemary, crushed

Directions:

In a large saucepan, cook bacon and ground beef until well done, breaking up the beef as it cooks. Drain off the fat.

Add in carrots, zucchini, garlic, onion and celery. Cook for about 5 minutes, stirring, or until the onions are translucent.

Add the bay leaf, basil and rosemary. Stir in tomatoes and beef broth. Bring to a boil, add in quinoa and chickpeas, reduce heat and simmer for about 20 minutes.

Serve hot.

Mediterranean Fish and Quinoa Soup

Serves: 4-5

Prep time: 30 min

Ingredients:

1 lb cod fillets, cubed

1 onion, chopped

3 tomatoes, chopped

1/2 cup quinoa, rinsed

1 red pepper, chopped

1 carrots, chopped

1/2 cup black olives, pitted and sliced

1 garlic clove, crushed

3 tbsp extra virgin olive oil

a pinch of cayenne pepper

1 bay leaf

1 tsp dried thyme

1 tsp dried dill

½ tsp pepper

½ cup white wine

4 cups water

salt and black pepper, to taste

1/2 cup fresh parsley, finely cut

Directions:

Heat the olive oil over medium heat and sauté the onion, red pepper, garlic and carrot until tender.

Stir in the cayenne pepper, bay leaf, herbs, salt and pepper. Add the white wine, water, quinoa and tomatoes and bring to a boil.

Reduce heat, cover, and cook for 10 minutes. Stir in olives and the fish and cook for another 10 minutes. Stir in parsley and serve hot.

Quinoa, Sweet Potato and Tomato Soup

Serves: 4

Prep time: 20 min

Ingredients:

½ cup quinoa, rinsed

1 onion, chopped

1 large sweet potato, peeled and diced

½ cup canned chickpeas, drained

1 cup baby spinach leaves

1 can tomatoes, drained and diced

3 cups vegetable broth

1 cup water

2 cloves garlic, chopped

1 tbsp grated fresh ginger

1 tsp cumin

1 tbsp paprika

2 tbsp extra virgin olive oil

Directions:

In a large soup pot, heat the olive oil over medium heat. Add the onions and garlic and sauté about 1-2 minutes, stirring. Add the sweet potato and sauté for another minute then add in the paprika, ginger and cumin.

Add water and broth, bring to a boil and stir in quinoa and tomatoes. Reduce heat to low, cover, and simmer about 15 minutes, or until the sweet potatoes are tender. Season with salt and black pepper to taste.

Blend the soup and return to the pot. Add the chickpeas and heat through, then add the spinach and cook until it wilts.

Leek and Quinoa Soup

Serves: 4-5

Prep time: 15 min

Ingredients:

½ cup quinoa, rinsed

3 leeks, white part only, sliced

3 garlic cloves, chopped

1 potato, cut in small cubes

½ cup canned chickpeas, drained

4 cups vegetable broth

1 cup milk

2 tbsp extra virgin olive oil

½ tsp ground coriander

1 tsp turmeric

salt and black pepper, to taste

Directions:

In a large soup pot, heat the olive oil over medium heat. Add the garlic and sauté for 1-2 minutes, stirring. Add in the spices and stir.

Add the broth and bring to the boil then stir in the quinoa, leeks, chickpeas and potato. Reduce heat and simmer, covered, for 15 minutes. Add in a cup of milk, stir, and simmer for 2 more minutes.

Red Lentil and Quinoa Soup

Serves: 4

Prep time: 20 min

Ingredients:

½ cup quinoa, rinsed

1 cup red lentils

5 cups water

1 onion, chopped

2-3 garlic cloves, chopped

½ red bell pepper, finely cut

1 small tomato, chopped

3 tbsp extra virgin olive oil

1 tsp ginger

1 tsp cumin

1 tbsp paprika

salt and black pepper, to taste

Directions:

In a large soup pot, heat the olive oil over medium heat. Add the onion, garlic and red pepper and sauté for 1-2 minutes, stirring. Add the paprika and spices and stir.

Add in the red lentils and quinoa, stir and add the water. Gently bring to the boil, then lower heat and simmer, covered for 15 minutes. Add the tomato and cook for five more minutes. Blend the soup, serve and enjoy!

Spinach and Quinoa Soup

Serves: 4-5

Prep time: 20 min

Ingredients:

½ cup quinoa, rinsed

1 onion, chopped

1 garlic clove, chopped

1 small zucchini, peeled and diced

1 tomato, diced

2 cups fresh spinach, cut

4 cups water

3 tbsp extra virgin olive oil

1 tbsp paprika

salt and pepper, to taste

1 cup Greek yogurt, to serve

Directions:

Heat olive oil in a deep soup pot over medium-high heat. Add onion and garlic and sauté for one minute, stirring constantly. Add in paprika and the zucchini, stir, and cook for 2-3 minutes more.

Add 4 cups of water and bring to a boil then add in spinach and quinoa. Stir and reduce heat. Simmer for 15 minutes then set aside to cool. Serve with a dollop of yogurt.

Vegetable Quinoa Soup

Serves: 4-5

Prep time: 20 min

Ingredients:

½ cup quinoa, rinsed

1 cup sliced leeks

1 garlic clove, chopped

½ carrot, diced

1 tomato, diced

1 small zucchini, diced

½ cup frozen green beans

4 cups water

1 tsp paprika

4 tbsp extra virgin olive oil

5-6 tbsp lemon juice, to serve

Directions:

Heat olive oil in a soup pot and gently sauté the leeks, garlic and carrot for one minute, stirring. Add in paprika, the zucchini, tomatoes, green beans and water.

Bring to a boil, stir in quinoa and lower heat to medium-low. Simmer for 15 minutes, or until the vegetables are tender. Serve with lemon juice.

Spicy Carrot and Quinoa Soup

Serves: 4-5

Prep time: 20 min

Ingredients:

4 carrots, chopped

1 small, chopped

1 garlic clove, crushed

4 cups vegetable broth

1/2 cup quinoa, rinsed

½ cup orange juice

3-4 tbsp extra virgin olive oil

1 tsp paprika

½ tsp ginger

salt and black pepper, to taste

1 cup yogurt, to serve

salt and black pepper, to taste

Directions:

Heat olive oil in a deep soup pot over medium-high heat. Gently sauté onion, garlic and carrots for 3-4 minutes, stirring. Add in paprika, ginger, orange juice, broth and quinoa.

Bring to the boil, reduce heat and simmer, covered, for 10 minutes.

Blend soup until smooth and return to pan. Cook over medium-high heat until heated through. Season with salt and pepper to taste and serve topped with yogurt.

Minted Pea and Quinoa Soup

Serves: 4

Prep time: 20 min

Ingredients:

1 16 oz bag frozen green peas

1 cup quinoa, rinsed

1 onion, chopped

3-4 garlic cloves, chopped

5 cups vegetable broth

2 tbsp dried mint leaves

3 tbsp extra virgin olive oil

1/4 cup yogurt, to serve

fresh dill, finely chopped, to serve

Directions:

Heat oil in a large saucepan over medium-high heat and sauté onion and garlic for 3-4 minutes.

Add in dried mint, peas, quinoa and vegetable broth and bring to a boil. Cover, reduce heat, and simmer for 15 minutes.

Remove from heat and set aside to cool slightly. Blend in batches, until smooth then return to saucepan over medium-low heat and cook until heated through.

Season with salt and pepper to taste and serve topped with yogurt and sprinkled with fresh dill.

Quinoa Main Dishes

Quinoa, Chicken and Mushroom Stew

Serves: 4-5

Prep time: 20-30 min

Ingredients:

2 cups cooked chicken

1 onion, chopped

2 cups mushrooms, chopped

1 carrot, chopped

1 cup quinoa, rinsed

2 cups vegetable broth

4 tbsp extra virgin olive oil

1 tsp oregano

1 cup fresh parsley, finely cut

Directions:

In a deep, heavy-bottomed saucepan, heat olive oil and gently sauté the onion, mushrooms and carrot for 4-5 minutes, stirring constantly.

Add in chicken, vegetable broth, and quinoa. Stir, season with salt, oregano and black pepper and bring to a boil.

Cover, reduce heat, and simmer for about 15 minutes, stirring from time to time. Sprinkle with parsley, set aside for a few minutes, and serve.

Apricot Chicken with Almonds and Quinoa

Serves: 4

Prep time: 45 min

Ingredients:

2 lb boneless chicken breasts or thighs, cut in 1-2 inch pieces

1 lb apricots, roughly chopped, pits removed and discarded

1 cup orange juice

1 cup quinoa, rinsed

1/4 cup blanched almonds

2 cups chicken broth

1 tsp ground cinnamon

1 tsp turmeric

salt and black pepper, to taste

Directions:

In a deep pan, combine orange juice with apricots, almonds, turmeric and cinnamon. Bring to a boil then reduce heat to medium-low and boil for 10 minutes or until the liquid is reduced by half.

Add in the chicken and chicken broth and bring to a boil. Stir in quinoa and simmer for 35 minutes or until cooked through.

Season to taste with salt and pepper to taste and serve.

Chicken Stew with Sweet Potatoes and Quinoa

Serves: 4

Prep time: 20 min

Ingredients:

2 lb boneless chicken thighs

2 lb sweet potatoes, peeled and cut into chunks

1 small onion, chopped

2-3 garlic cloves

1 cup quinoa, rinsed

1 cup chicken broth

1 can crushed tomatoes

1 cup roasted peanuts

1 tsp ground ginger

1 tsp ground coriander

salt and black pepper, to taste

Directions:

Heat the vegetable oil in a large soup pot set over medium-high heat. Salt the chicken pieces well, pat them dry and brown them in the oil.

Add in the onions, garlic and ginger and sauté for 1-2 minutes, stirring often.

Stir in the chicken broth, tomatoes, sweet potatoes, peanuts, sugar, coriander and bring to a boil. Simmer for 15 minutes then add quinoa and cook for 15 minutes more or until cooked through.

Season to taste with salt and pepper to taste, and serve.

Lazy Mustard Chicken with Quinoa

Serves: 4

Prep time: 45 min

Ingredients:

2 lb chicken thighs

2 garlic cloves, crushed

1/2 cup quinoa, rinsed

1 cup chicken broth

1/4 to 1/3 cup Dijon mustard

2 tbsp honey

1 tsp dried rosemary

2 tbsp extra virgin olive oil

salt and pepper, to taste

Directions:

Gently heat the olive oil in a shallow casserole dish over medium-low heat and sauté the garlic for about a minute, stirring.

In a medium bowl, whisk together the mustard, chicken broth, honey and dried rosemary.

Season the chicken pieces with salt and black pepper to taste and lay them skin-side up. Spoon the honey mustard sauce over the chicken.

Bake in a preheated to 350 F oven for 30 minutes. Add in quinoa, stir, and bake until the chicken is cooked through, about 15 more minutes.

Beef with Quinoa and Melting Onions

Serves: 6

Prep time: 120 min

Ingredients:

2 lb stewing beef

1 cup quinoa, rinsed

4 large onions, sliced

3 garlic cloves, chopped

1 bay leaf

2 cups chicken broth

4 tbsp extra virgin olive oil

1 tsp cinnamon

1/2 tsp ginger powder

salt and black pepper, to taste

Directions:

Heat olive oil in a large saucepan and brown the beef. Add in the onions and garlic and saute for 2-3 minutes, stirring.

Add in cinnamon, ginger, the bay leaf, black pepper and chicken broth. Bring to a boil.

Reduce heat to low, cover, and simmer for about 90 minutes, stirring occasionally. When the beef is almost done, add in quinoa, stir and simmer for 20 minutes more.

Ground Beef, Quinoa and Cabbage Casserole

Serves: 4-5

Prep time: 50 min

Ingredients:

1 lb ground beef

1 cup quinoa, rinsed

1/2 cabbage, shredded

1/2 onion, chopped

2 leeks, white part only, chopped

1 tomato, diced

1 tbsp paprika

1/2 tsp cumin

½ tsp black pepper

4 tbsp extra virgin olive oil

salt, to taste

Directions:

In a deep saucepan, sauté the onion and leeks in olive oil until tender. Add in the ground beef, quinoa, tomato, paprika, cumin, salt and black pepper. Stir very well.

Place shredded cabbage on the bottom of an ovenproof baking dish. Cover with beef and quinoa mixture. Cover with a lid or aluminum foil and bake at 325 F for 40 minutes.

Citrus Pork with Quinoa

Serves 5-6

Prep time: 80 min

Ingredients:

2 lb pork shoulder, cut into 1 inch chunks

1 cup quinoa, rinsed

1 cup orange juice

1 cup water

1 large carrot, chopped

6-7 spring onions, finely cut

1-2 garlic cloves, chopped

1 tbsp lemon zest

1/2 tsp cumin

3 tbsp extra virgin olive oil

Directions:

Heat the olive oil in a large skillet over medium-high heat. Working in batches, brown the pieces of pork shoulder.

Add in the carrots, garlic, lemon zest, cumin, salt and black pepper to taste. Stir, and cook for 1-2 minutes, stirring.

Add the orange juice and water, bring to a simmer and cook for 40 minutes.

Stir in quinoa and spring onions and cook for 15 minutes more.

Spicy Pork Stew with Leeks and Quinoa

Serves 5-6

Prep time: 80 min

Ingredients:

2 lb pork shoulder, cut into 1 inch chunks

1 cup quinoa, rinsed

1 lb leeks, cut

1 large carrot, chopped

1 red pepper, cut

4-5 garlic cloves, chopped

1 tbsp paprika

1 tsp hot paprika

3 tbsp extra virgin olive oil

2 tbsp tomato paste, dissolved in 1/3 cup water

Directions:

Heat the olive oil in a large pot over medium-high heat. Working in batches, brown the pieces of pork shoulder.

Add in the carrot, pepper, leeks, garlic, salt, black pepper to taste and paprika. Stir, and add the tomato paste. Bring to a simmer and cook for one hour.

Stir in quinoa and cook for 15 minutes more.

Comforting Lamb and Quinoa Shepherd's Stew

Serves: 4-5

Prep time: 60 min

Ingredients:

4 shoulder lamb chops, de-boned and cubed

1 cup quinoa

1 ½ cups chicken broth

1 onion, finely cut

2 garlic cloves, chopped

2 red peppers, chopped

1 carrot, cut into bite size pieces

1 turnip, cut into bite size pieces

6-7 white mushrooms, chopped

1-2 tomatoes, diced

2 tbsp extra virgin olive oil

1 tbsp paprika

1 bay leaf

1 tbsp thyme

Directions:

Wash quinoa very well, drain and set aside.

In a large soup pot or casserole dish, heat the oil over medium heat and brown the meat for 8-10 minutes. Add the onion, bell peppers and garlic and cook until softened, about 3 minutes. Stir in paprika, the bay leaf and thyme. Add the other vegetables and mushrooms and cook for 1-2 minutes, stirring.

Add in the broth, bring to the boil and simmer for 30 minutes. Stir in the quinoa and simmer for 15 minutes more.

Tuna and Quinoa Patties

Serves: 7

Prep time: 20-30 min

Ingredients:

2 6 oz cans tuna

1/2 cup cooked quinoa

1 large egg

1 tbsp Dijon mustard

2 tbsp lemon juice

2-3 spring onions, finely chopped

½ cup fresh parsley, finely chopped

1/4 cup extra virgin olive oil

1 tsp salt

black pepper, to taste

Directions:

In a medium bowl, mix together the tuna, mustard, quinoa, lemon juice, spring onions, parsley, and salt. Add in freshly ground black pepper and the egg.

Using your hands, form batter into burgers. Bake in a preheated to 375F oven for 7-8 minutes or until golden.

Vegetable Quinoa Stew

Serves: 4-5

Prep time: 25 min

Ingredients:

1 cup quinoa

1 ½ cup water

1 onion, finely cut

2 red bell peppers, chopped

1 zucchini, peeled and chopped

1 cup fresh green peas

5-6 green beans

1 tomato, chopped

1 potato, peeled and diced

2 garlic cloves, chopped

1 tbsp paprika

3 tbsp extra virgin olive oil

salt, to taste

½ cup fresh dill, finely cut, to serve

Directions:

Rinse the quinoa very well in a sieve under running water and set aside to drain.

Heat olive oil in large saucepan over medium-high heat. Add in the onion and sauté for 1-2 minutes. Add the garlic, paprika, bell pepper, green peas, green beans and zucchini. Cook, stirring occasionally, for 5 minutes then add the tomato, the potato, and the water.

Bring to the boil and add in quinoa. Stir, cover, and cook for 20 minutes. Season with salt to taste and serve sprinkled with dill.

Eggplant and Quinoa Stew

Serves: 4-5

Prep time: 25 min

Ingredients:

1 cup quinoa

1 ½ cups water

1 large eggplant, peeled and diced

1 cup canned tomatoes, drained and diced

1 zucchini, diced

5-6 black olives, pitted and halved

1 onion, chopped

4 garlic cloves, chopped

1 tbsp tomato paste

3 tbsp extra virgin olive oil

1 tsp paprika

salt and black pepper, to taste

½ cup parsley leaves, finely cut, to serve

Directions:

Rinse the quinoa very well in a fine sieve under running water and set aside to drain.

Gently sauté onions, garlic and eggplant in olive oil on medium-high heat for 5-6 minutes. Add paprika and tomato paste and stir for 1-2 minutes. Add in the rest of the vegetables and the water; and bring to the boil.

Stir in quinoa, lower heat and simmer, covered, for 20 minutes.

Sprinkle with parsley and serve.

Easy Moroccan Vegetable Stew with Quinoa

Serves: 6

Prep time: 25 min

Ingredients:

1 large onion, chopped

2 garlic cloves, chopped

1 cup quinoa

2 cups vegetable broth

1 cup canned chickpeas, drained

1 cup canned tomatoes, diced and undrained

1 carrot, chopped

1 cup baby spinach leaves

¼ cup dried prunes

¼ cup dried apricots

1 zucchini, quartered lengthwise and chopped

½ cup almonds, coarsely chopped

3 tbsp extra virgin olive oil

1 tsp grated ginger

1 tsp ground cinnamon

Directions:

In a large soup pot or casserole dish, heat the oil over medium heat. Add in the onion, ginger, garlic and cinnamon and sauté for 2-3 minutes, or until the onion has softened.

Stir in vegetable broth, chickpeas, tomatoes, carrots, apricots and prunes and bring to a boil. Add quinoa and the zucchini, reduce heat and simmer, covered, for 15 minutes. Add in the baby spinach and cook until it wilts. Add the almonds, stir, and serve.

Zucchini and Quinoa Stew

Serves: 4-5

Prep time: 20 min

Ingredients:

1 cup quinoa, rinsed

2 cups vegetable broth

1 onion, finely chopped

3 garlic cloves, chopped

4 zucchinis, peeled and diced

1 cup fresh dill, finely cut

3 tbsp extra virgin olive oil

salt, to taste

Directions:

In a deep saucepan, heat olive oil and gently sauté the onion and garlic for 1-2 minutes. Add the diced zucchinis and sauté for 5-6 minutes, stirring.

Add in vegetable broth and bring to a boil then stir in quinoa, dill and salt to taste. Lower heat, cover, and simmer for 15 minutes.

Curried Quinoa with Raisins and Apples

Serves: 4-5

Prep time: 20 min

Ingredients:

1 cup cooked quinoa

1 large apple, peeled and chopped

½ cup raisins

½ cup coarsely chopped almonds or walnuts

4-5 green onions, finely cut

1 tsp curry powder

¼ tsp ground turmeric

2 tbsp extra virgin olive oil

1 tbsp apple cider vinegar

salt and black pepper, to taste

Directions:

In a large bowl, toss together the apple, raisins, almonds and green onions. Add the cooked quinoa and toss to combine.

In a small saucepan, warm the olive oil, curry and turmeric for 1-2 minutes. Remove from heat and let cool for one minute. Add the vinegar and pour this mixture over the quinoa mixture. Stir until all ingredients are well coated.

Quick Quinoa Chili

Serves: 4-5

Prep time: 20-25 min

Ingredients:

1 cup quinoa, rinsed

2 cups vegetable broth

1 large onion, finely cut

3 cloves garlic, chopped

1 green bell pepper, chopped

1 can diced tomatoes

1 can black beans, well rinsed and drained

1 tbsp paprika

1 tsp chili powder

1 tsp ground cumin

2 tbsp extra virgin olive oil

¼ cup chopped fresh coriander, to serve

Directions:

In a large soup pot or casserole dish, heat the oil over medium heat. Add the onion, bell pepper and garlic and sauté until softened, about 3 minutes.

Stir in the chili powder, cumin and paprika and sauté for another minute. Add in vegetable broth, tomatoes, beans and quinoa and stir to combine well.

Bring to a boil then reduce heat to low and simmer, covered, for about 15 minutes. Serve sprinkled with fresh coriander.

Spicy Quinoa and Spinach Stew

Serves: 4

Prep time: 40 min

Ingredients:

1 onion, chopped

3 garlic cloves, chopped

1 cup quinoa, rinsed

2 tomatoes, diced

1 1 lb bag baby spinach

a handful of blanched almonds

2 cups vegetable broth

1 tbsp hot chili paste

½ tsp cumin

salt and pepper, to taste

Directions:

Heat olive oil in a large saucepan over medium-high heat. Gently sauté onion and garlic for 4-5 minutes, or until tender. Add in spices and stir.

Add water, quinoa, tomatoes and almonds then bring to a boil. Reduce heat to low and simmer, partially covered, for 15 minutes.

Stir in the chili paste and spinach to and cook until the spinach wilts. Season with salt and pepper to taste and serve.

Mediterranean Style Quinoa Stew

Serves: 4-5

Prep time: 20 min

Ingredients:

1 onion, chopped

3 garlic cloves, chopped

1 large carrot, chopped

1 sweet potato, peeled and chopped

4-5 dates, pitted and chopped

1 cup spinach, chopped

1 15 oz can tomatoes, diced and undrained

1 cup quinoa, rinsed

2 cups vegetable broth

1 tbsp ground cumin

½ tsp ground turmeric

½ teaspoon salt

3 tbsp extra virgin olive oil

½ cup chopped cilantro, to serve

grated lemon zest, to serve

Directions:

Heat olive oil in a large saucepan over medium-high heat. Gently sauté onion, garlic and carrots for 4-5 minutes, or until tender.

Stir in spices and all other ingredients except the spinach. Bring to a boil, cover, reduce heat, and simmer for 20 minutes, or until the sweet potatoes are tender.

Add in spinach, stir, and cook until it wilts. Serve sprinkled with chopped cilantro and lemon zest.

Quinoa, Leek and Olive Stew

Serves: 4-5

Prep time: 20 min

Ingredients:

5 cups sliced leeks

25-30 black olives, pitted and halved

1 cup quinoa, rinsed

2 cups water

1 cup grated Parmesan cheese

4 tbsp extra virgin olive oil

salt and black pepper, to taste

Directions:

In a deep baking dish, heat olive oil and sauté the leeks for 2-3 minutes, stirring. Add in the water, quinoa and olives.

Season with salt and black pepper and bake in a preheated to 350 F oven for 15 minutes. Sprinkle with Parmesan cheese and bake for 3-4 minutes more.

Quinoa Stuffed Eggplants

Serves: 4

Prep time: 35 min

Ingredients:

4 eggplants

1 cup cooked quinoa

1 tomatoes, grated

2 onions, finely chopped

1 carrot, grated

4-5 cloves garlic

1 bay leaf

1/2 cup fresh parsley, finely cut

1 tbsp paprika

1 cup grated Parmesan cheese

1/4 cup extra virgin olive oil

1 tsp salt

Directions:

Wash and peel the eggplants. Cut them in half lengthwise and carefully hollow them out. Salt them and leave them aside for 15 minutes.

In a skillet, heat the olive oil and gently sauté the chopped onions, garlic, carrot and tomatoes, stirring. Add in the quinoa, parsley, the bay leaf, black pepper, to taste, and salt.

Rinse the eggplants and stuff them with the vegetable quinoa mixture. Arrange them in a baking dish. Top with a slice of tomato and sprinkle with Parmesan cheese.

Bake in a preheated to 350 F oven until the eggplants are soft to the touch. Serve room temperature.

Quinoa Breakfasts and Desserts

Hearty Quinoa and Spinach Breakfast Casserole

Serves: 4

Prep time: 30 min

Ingredients:

1 cup cooked quinoa

3-4 spring onions, finely chopped

5 oz frozen chopped spinach, thawed and squeezed dry

½ zucchini, peeled and shredded

5 eggs

1/2 cup milk

4 tbsp extra virgin olive oil

salt and black pepper, to taste

1 cup cheddar cheese, grated

Directions:

In a large bowl combine eggs, milk, salt and pepper.

In a deep casserole dish heat the olive oil. Cook the onions, zucchini and spinach, stirring constantly, until lightly cooked. Add in the quinoa and combine everything well. Pour the egg mixture over and then top with cheddar cheese.

Bake in a preheated to 350 F oven for 20 minutes.

Quick Quinoa Vegetable Scramble

Serves: 4

Prep time: 10 min

Ingredients:

1/2 cup cooked quinoa

1/2 small onion, chopped

2 tomatoes, diced

1 large red pepper, chopped

5 eggs

1/2 cup crumbled feta

4 tbsp extra virgin olive oil

black pepper, to taste

salt, to taste

Directions:

In a large pan, sauté onion over medium heat for 1-2 minutes, stirring. Add in tomatoes and red pepper and cook until the mixture is almost dry.

Stir in quinoa, feta and eggs and cook until well mixed and not too liquid.

Season with black pepper and serve.

Coconut and Quinoa Banana Pudding

Serves 4

Prep time: 15 min

Ingredients:

1 cup quinoa

3 cups coconut milk

3 ripe bananas

1/4 cup flaked unsweetened coconut

4 tbsp sugar

1 tsp vanilla extract

Directions:

Wash and cook quinoa according to package directions. When ready remove from heat and set aside.

In a separate bowl blend sugar, milk and bananas until smooth. Add to the quinoa. Heat over medium heat, string, until creamy. Stir in vanilla and coconut flakes and serve warm.

Cranberry Quinoa Breakfast

Serves 2

Prep time: 15 min

Ingredients:

½ cup quinoa

1 cup milk

2-3 tbsp honey, optional

1 tsp cinnamon

½ tsp vanilla

1 tsp ground flaxseed

2 tbsp walnuts or almonds, chopped

2 tbsp dried cranberries

Directions:

Rinse quinoa and drain. Combine milk, quinoa and flaxseed into a saucepan. Bring to a boil, add in cinnamon and vanilla and simmer for about 15 minutes.

When done, place a portion of the quinoa into a bowl, drizzle with honey, and top with cranberries and crushed walnuts.

Berry Quinoa and Chia Seed Breakfast

Serves 2

Prep time: 15 min

Ingredients:

½ cup quinoa

11/2 cups milk

2 tbsp chia seeds

¼ cup fresh blueberries or raspberries

2 tbsp pistachios, silvered

Directions:

Combine quinoa and chia seeds with milk and bring to a boil. Cover, reduce heat and simmer for 15 minutes.

When ready, serve into bowls and top with fresh berries and pistachios.

Quinoa and Date Cookies

Serves 8-10

Prep time: 15-20 min

Ingredients:

1/2 cup almond flour

1/2 cup cooked quinoa

1/3 cup brown sugar

½ cup butter

4 tbsp tahini

16 dates, pitted and chopped

1 tsp baking soda

½ tsp vanilla extract

Directions:

Preheat oven to 350 F degrees. Combine sugar, tahini and butter stirring until creamy. Add in remaining ingredients. Mix very well.

Spoon rounded teaspoonfuls of dough onto cookie sheets. Bake for 10-12 minutes, or until cookies start to turn golden brown.

Quinoa, Chocolate and Banana Muffins

Serves 12

Prep time: 20 min

Ingredients:

11/2 cups cooked quinoa

1 ripe banana, mashed

¼ cup sugar

⅓ cup unsweetened applesauce

4 eggs

1/2 cup milk

1/2 cup cocoa powder

3 tbsp sunflower oil

1 tsp vanilla

1 tbsp baking powder

½ tsp baking soda

½ tsp salt

Directions:

Preheat oven to 350 F. Combine all wet ingredients and mix well. In a separate bowl combine dry ingredients. Add dry ingredients to wet ingredients gently stirring.

Grease 12 muffin tins. Spoon dough evenly into cups. Bake for 15-16 minutes until you press them and they spring back.

Quinoa Fruit Salad

Serves 2

Prep time: 15 min

Ingredients:

¼ cup quinoa

1 apple, diced

1 pear, diced

½ cup blueberries

1/2 cup chopped almonds

2 tbsp honey

1 tsp cinnamon

1 tbsp lemon juice

Directions:

Wash and cook quinoa according to package directions. Set aside to cool.

Combine fruit in a deep bowl. Add in quinoa and toss to combine.

Combine lemon juice, honey and cinnamon and drizzle on the fruit salad. Serve sprinkled with chopped almonds.

Chocolate Quinoa Cake

Serves 12

Prep time: 45 min

Ingredients:

2 cups cooked quinoa, cold

1 1/4 cups white sugar

3 eggs

2 tbsp flaxseed

3/4 cup melted butter

1/2 cup milk

1 cup cocoa powder

1 tbsp baking powder

1 tsp baking soda

1/2 teaspoon salt

1/2 cup chocolate chips

1/2 cup raisins

1 1/2 teaspoons vanilla extract

1 tsp rum aroma

Directions:

Blend butter, eggs, milk, quinoa, flaxseed and vanilla extract together in a blender until smooth.

Combine sugar, cocoa powder, baking powder, baking soda, and salt in deep bowl. Stir quinoa mixture into sugar mixture until batter is well combined. Add chocolate chips and raisins.

Pour into the prepared pan and bake in a preheated to 350 F oven until a toothpick inserted in the cake comes out clean, 40-45 minutes. Let the cake cool on a wire rack.

Quinoa Vanilla Pancakes

Serves: 4

Prep time: 15 min

Ingredients:

1 cup cooked quinoa

2 large eggs, beaten

1/2 tsp baking powder

1/2 tsp salt

1 tbsp sunflower oil

1 tbsp vanilla extract

maple syrup, honey or fruit, to serve

Directions:

Combine all ingredients into a medium bowl.

Heat a nonstick skillet over medium to medium-low heat. Drop batter by heaping tablespoonfuls into the skillet and cook for 3-4 minutes on the first side until pancakes are set. Flip and cook for another 1-2 minutes.

Serve with maple syrup, honey, nut butter or fresh fruit.

Easy Quinoa Crackers

Serves 2

Prep time: 70 min

Ingredients:

2 cups cooked quinoa

1 cup ground flaxseed

2 tbsp sesame seeds

1 tbsp honey

1 tsp salt

1 cup water

3 tbsp extra virgin olive oil

1 tsp garlic powder (optional)

1/2 tsp dried oregano (optional)

Directions:

Throughly mix together all ingredients in a large bowl.

Place the dough on a lined baking sheet and with wet hands, flatten the dough. Slip the parchment off of the baking sheet, cover the length of the dough with plastic wrap and roll out the dough with a rolling pin to a ¼ inch thickness.

Bake at 350 F for 35 minutes or until the parchment paper easily pulls away and the dough is cooked but not crisp yet. Flip the cracker over, gently remove the parchment paper and cut into squares. Bake for another 35 minutes, or until the crackers are nice and crisp.

FREE BONUS RECIPES: 20 Superfood Paleo and Vegan Smoothies for Vibrant Health and Easy Weight Loss

Kale and Kiwi Smoothie

Serves: 2

Prep time: 2-3 min

Ingredients:

2-3 ice cubes

1 cup orange juice

1 small pear, peeled and chopped

2 kiwi, peeled and chopped

2-3 kale leaves

2-3 dates, pitted

Directions:

Combine all ingredients in a high speed blender and blend until smooth.

Delicious Broccoli Smoothie

Serves: 2

Prep time: 2-3 min

Ingredients:

2-3 frozen broccoli florets

1 cup coconut milk

1 banana, peeled and chopped

1 cup pineapple, cut

1 peach, chopped

1 tsp cinnamon

Directions:

Combine all ingredients in a high speed blender and blend until smooth.

Papaya Smoothie

Serves: 2

Prep time: 2-3 min

Ingredients:

2-3 frozen broccoli florets

1 cup orange juice

1 small ripe avocado, peeled, cored and diced

1 cup papaya

1 cup fresh strawberries

Directions:

Combine all ingredients in a high speed blender and blend until smooth.

Beet and Papaya Smoothie

Serves: 2

Prep time: 2-3 min

Ingredients:

3-4 ice cubes

1 cup orange juice

1 banana, peeled and chopped

1 cup papaya

1 small beet, peeled and cut

Directions:

Combine all ingredients in a high speed blender and blend until smooth.

Lean Green Smoothie

Serves: 2

Prep time: 2-3 min

Ingredients:

1 frozen banana, chopped

1 cup orange juice

2-3 kale leaves, stems removed

1 small cucumber, peeled and chopped

1/2 cup fresh parsley leaves

½ tsp grated ginger

Directions:

Combine all ingredients in a high speed blender and blend until smooth.

Easy Antioxidant Smoothie

Serves: 2

Prep time: 2-3 min

Ingredients:

2-3 frozen broccoli florets

1 cup orange juice

2 plums, cut

1 cup raspberries

1 tsp ginger powder

Directions:

Combine all ingredients in a high speed blender and blend until smooth.

Healthy Purple Smoothie

Serves: 2

Prep time: 2-3 min

Ingredients:

2-3 frozen broccoli florets

1 cup water

1/2 avocado, peeled and chopped

3 plums, chopped

1 cup blueberries

Directions:

Combine all ingredients in a high speed blender and blend until smooth.

Mom's Favorite Kale Smoothie

Serves: 2

Prep time: 2-3 min

Ingredients:

2-3 ice cubes

1½ cup orange juice

1 green small apple, cut

½ cucumber, chopped

2-3 leaves kale

½ cup raspberries

Directions:

Combine all ingredients in a high speed blender and blend until smooth.

Creamy Green Smoothie

Serves: 2

Prep time: 2-3 min

Ingredients:

1 frozen banana

1 cup coconut milk

1 small pear, chopped

1 cup baby spinach

1 cup grapes

1 tbsp coconut butter

1 tsp vanilla extract

Directions:

Combine all ingredients in a high speed blender and blend until smooth.

Strawberry and Arugula Smoothie

Serves: 2

Prep time: 2-3 min

Ingredients:

2 cups frozen strawberries

1 cup unsweetened almond milk

10-12 arugula leaves

1/2 tsp ground cinnamon

Directions:

Combine ice, almond milk, strawberries, arugula and cinnamon in a high speed blender. Blend until smooth and serve.

Emma's Amazing Smoothie

Serves: 2

Prep time: 2-3 min

Ingredients:

1 frozen banana, chopped

1 cup orange juice

1 large nectarine, sliced

1/2 zucchini, peeled and chopped

2-3 dates, pitted

Directions:

Combine all ingredients in a high speed blender and blend until smooth.

Good-To-Go Morning Smoothie

Serves: 2

Prep time: 2-3 min

Ingredients:

1 cup frozen strawberries

1 cup apple juice

1 banana, chopped

1 cup raw asparagus, chopped

1 tbsp ground flaxseed

Directions:

Combine all ingredients in a high speed blender and blend until smooth.

Endless Energy Smoothie

Serves: 2

Prep time: 2-3 min

Ingredients:

1 frozen banana, chopped

11/2 cup green tea

1 cup chopped pineapple

2 raw asparagus spears, chopped

1 lime, juiced

1 tbsp chia seeds

Directions:

Combine all ingredients in a high speed blender and blend until smooth.

High-fibre Fruit Smoothie

Serves: 2

Prep time: 2-3 min

Ingredients:

1 frozen banana, chopped

1 cup orange juice

2 cups chopped papaya

1 cup shredded cabbage

1 tbsp chia seeds

Directions:

Combine all ingredients in a high speed blender and blend until smooth.

Nutritious Green Smoothie

Serves: 2

Prep time: 2-3 min

Ingredients:

2-3 frozen broccoli florets

1 cup apple juice

1 large pear, chopped

1 kiwi, peeled and chopped

1 cup spinach leaves

1-2 dates, pitted

Directions:

Combine all ingredients in a high speed blender and blend until smooth.

Apricot, Strawberry and Banana Smoothie

Serves: 2

Prep time: 2-3 min

Ingredients:

1 frozen banana

11/2 cup almond milk

5 dried apricots

1 cup fresh strawberries

Directions:

Combine all ingredients in a high speed blender and blend until smooth.

Spinach and Green Apple Smoothie

Serves: 2

Prep time: 2-3 min

Ingredients:

3-4 ice cubes

1 cup unsweetened almond milk

1 banana, peeled and chopped

2 green apples, peeled and chopped

1 cup raw spinach leaves

3-4 dates, pitted

1 tsp grated ginger

Directions:

Combine all ingredients in a high speed blender and blend until smooth.

Superfood Blueberry Smoothie

Serves: 2

Prep time: 2-3 min

Ingredients:

2-3 cubes frozen spinach

1 cup green tea

1 banana

2 cups blueberries

1 tbsp ground flaxseed

Directions:

Combine all ingredients in a high speed blender and blend until smooth.

Zucchini and Blueberry Smoothie

Serves: 2

Prep time: 2-3 min

Ingredients:

1 cup frozen blueberries

1 cup unsweetened almond milk

1 banana

1 zucchini, peeled and chopped

Directions:

Combine all ingredients in a high speed blender and blend until smooth.

Tropical Spinach Smoothie

Serves: 2

Prep time: 2-3 min

Ingredients:

1/2 cup crushed ice or 3-4 ice cubes

1 cup coconut milk

1 mango, peeled and diced

1 cup fresh spinach leaves

4-5 dates, pitted

1/2 tsp vanilla extract

Directions:

Combine all ingredients in a high speed blender and blend until smooth.

About the Author

Alissa Grey is a fitness and nutrition enthusiast who loves to teach people about losing weight and feeling better about themselves. She lives in a small French village in the foothills of a beautiful mountain range with her husband, three teenage kids, two free spirited dogs, and various other animals.

Alissa Grey is incredibly lucky to be able to cook and eat natural foods, mostly grown nearby, something she's done since she was a teenager. She enjoys yoga, running, reading, hanging out with her family, and growing organic vegetables and herbs.

If you want to see other delicious and healthy family recipes that she has published you can check out her Author Page on Amazon.

32407811R00063

Printed in Great Britain
by Amazon